The Three Billy Goats Gruff

Story retold by Janet Brown
Illustrations by Ken Morton

High on a mountain side live three billy goats called Gruff. All day long they eat grass and play in the sunshine, and at night they sleep happily under the stars.

Where do the three billy goats live?

One day, the third billy goat Gruff says, "We've eaten our field bare. Let's go further up the mountain and try to find some sweeter grass."

So off they go.

Soon they come to a river. On the other side of the river is the richest, greenest meadow the billy goats Gruff have ever seen. Their mouths begin to water. They imagine how fat they will grow.

Why do the billy goats want to get across the river?

Now, in order to get to the meadow the three billy goats Gruff have to cross the river. Over the river is a long, wooden bridge. And under the bridge lives a mean old troll. Whenever he hears someone trying to cross the bridge, he pops up his big, ugly head and gobbles them up!

So nobody ever crosses the bridge.

Why doesn't anyone ever dare to cross the bridge?

"I'm not afraid," says the first billy goat Gruff. He begins to tiptoe over the bridge but his hooves make a great noise – *trip trap trip trap*!

Up pops the ugly head of the mean old troll! "Who's that trip-trapping over my bridge?" he roars.

The first billy goat Gruff begins to shiver and shake with fear. "Please don't gobble me up!" he begs. "I'm not very big, just skin and bone. My big brother is coming behind me. Why not eat him up instead?"

"Good idea!" says the troll, smacking his lips.

And the first billy goat Gruff runs safely to the other side.

Why does the troll allow the first billy goat to cross the bridge?

The second billy goat Gruff sees his little brother running about in the juicy meadow across the river.

"I'm not afraid either," he says. He begins to tiptoe over the bridge but his hooves make an even greater noise – *Trip Trap Trip Trap*!

Up pops the ugly head of the mean old troll! "Who's that trip-trapping over my bridge?" he roars.

The second billy goat Gruff begins to quiver and quake with fear. "Please don't gobble me up!" he pleads. "I'm not very big, just hair and gristle. My big brother is coming behind me. Why not eat him up instead?"

"Good idea!" says the troll, smacking his lips.

And the second billy goat runs safely to the other side.

How does the second billy goat describe himself to the troll?

Now the third billy goat Gruff is almost fully grown. He is already quite fat and his horns are long and sharp. Instead of tiptoeing across the bridge, he begins to stamp across it – TRIP TRAP TRIP TRAP, THUMP THUMP THUMP!

Up pops the ugly head of the mean old troll! "Who's that stamping over my bridge?" he roars.

"It's me!" yells the third billy goat Gruff. "I'm very big, all juicy and fat. And there's no one coming behind me!"

The troll climbs out from under the bridge. "Then I'm going to gobble you up!" he roars, and smacks his lips.

What noise do the third billy goat's hooves make
as he crosses the bridge?

The troll stands on one end of the bridge. The third billy goat Gruff stands at the other end of the bridge. Then they rush at each other!

The troll is strong but the third billy goat Gruff is stronger. The troll has big fists but the third billy goat Gruff has big horns. They meet with a great CRASH! and the troll is sent flying off the bridge and into the river.

What happens to the troll when he rushes at
the third billy goat Gruff?

The oldest billy goat Gruff trots across the bridge to join his brothers. They stand at the edge of the river and look into the deep water. But they cannot see the troll.

Soon the villagers arrive. They are so happy that the troll has gone that they start to dance. *Tippety trip trap, tippety trip trap* go their feet on the bridge, all night long!

What do the villagers do on the bridge now that the troll has gone?

And the three billy goats Gruff eat the rich, green grass of the meadow and soon grow very fat indeed!

On a piece of paper practise writing these words:

crash

mountain

forest

bridge

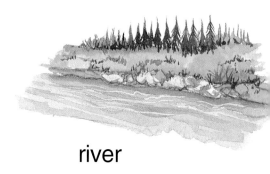

river